Col

Series ed

A library

language, and for reluctant nati...

levels of difficulty. Structure, vocabulary, idiom and sentence length are
all controlled according to principles laid down in detail in A Guide to
Collins English Library. A list of the books follows. Numbers after each
title indicate the level at which the book is written: 1 has a basic
vocabulary of 300 words and appropriate structures, 2 : 600 words, 3 :
1000 words, 4 : 1500 words, 5 : 2000 words and 6 : 2500 words.

Collins English Library   Level 2

TWO
ROMAN STORIES
from Shakespeare

Simplified and retold by Margery Morris

Illustrations by Campbell Kennedy

Collins: London and Glasgow

Published in Great Britain by
William Collins Sons and Co Ltd
Glasgow G4 0NB

Printed by Martin's of Berwick

First published in Collins English Library, 1979
Reprinted: 1982, 1984, 1985, 1987, 1989

We are grateful to Reg Wilson Photography
for permission to reproduce the photograph
which appears on the cover.

ISBN 0 00 370127 1

Julius Caesar

Shall Rome Have a King?

Julius Caesar, the great Roman soldier, came home from a war. The people of Rome took a holiday. They all came out into the streets to see Caesar, and to enjoy the holiday games and sport.

But there were some Romans who didn't enjoy the holiday. They were afraid; they thought Julius Caesar would become king of Rome, and they didn't want that. Under a king, the Roman people would not be free, as they were now. Most of the people, the workers, didn't understand this. They liked Caesar and they liked holidays and they were ready to have a king.

On this holiday, Caesar, with his wife Calpurnia, and some of his friends, Antony, Brutus, Cassius and Casca, walked through the streets.

A fortune-teller, a man who could see the future, called out, "Caesar! Listen!"

"I'm listening," said Caesar.

"Danger," said the fortune-teller. "Danger, Caesar. The 15th day of March, the Ides of March, will be dangerous for you."

Caesar laughed. "Leave him," he said. "He knows nothing."

Caesar moved on. Cassius stood still. He said to Brutus, "Are you going to see the games?"

"No," said Brutus. "I'm not like Antony. He loves sport, but I don't. You go, Cassius, if you want to."

Cassius didn't move. "Brutus," he said, "you seem unfriendly. What's wrong? Have I done something wrong?"

"No, no, Cassius," said Brutus. "I have a lot of unhappy thoughts, that's all."

Just then there was a noise from the sportsfield.

"Listen," said Brutus. "What's that? Perhaps the people are asking Caesar to be king."

"Don't you want that?"

"Caesar's my dear friend," said Brutus. "But I don't want Rome to have a king."

Cassius looked closely at him. Then he said, "Who is Caesar? What is he? The people seem to think he's a god. He's not. He's a tired, sick old man."

There was another loud noise from the sportsfield. Both men listened.

"I have always been free," said Cassius. "And you have, too."

"Cassius," said Brutus, "I know what you mean. But don't say any more now. Give me time. Let me think."

Brutus turned to go, but he saw Caesar, and stopped.

"The games are over," he said. "Caesar's coming back."

"Casca will tell us what has happened," said Cassius. "Stop him as he passes us."

Caesar saw Cassius and Brutus. He said to his friend Antony, "I don't like that Cassius. He thinks too much, and never smiles. He has cold eyes. Men like him are dangerous."

"No, no, Caesar," said Antony, "Cassius isn't

dangerous. He's a good Roman, and he loves you."

"I don't think he does," said Caesar.

Caesar moved on with Calpurnia, and Brutus stopped Casca.

"What is it?" said Casca shortly.

"What happened at the games?"

"They wanted Caesar to be king. They asked him three times."

"And Caesar....?"

"Caesar said 'No.' But he didn't want to say it."

"Didn't he?"

"No," said Casca. "He wants to be king. And I'll tell you something else. Two men took down some pictures of Caesar from the walls. Now they're both dead. Goodbye."

Casca went. Brutus said, "I must go, too. Tomorrow Caesar's going to sit with the other Roman leaders at the Capitol. The people will ask him for what they want."

"Yes."

"Come to my house early tomorrow, Cassius."

"I will."

Brutus walked away. Cassius thought, "You're a good man, Brutus, but I think we can use you. We must use you. The people think that Brutus can do no wrong."

Cassius began to walk home. "It's strange," he thought, "Caesar doesn't like me. But he loves Brutus. It's very strange that Brutus is ready to kill him."

The Night of the Storm

That night there was a great storm over Rome. Neither Cassius nor Casca could sleep, and both went out into the city. They met in the darkness.

"This storm! Something bad is going to happen," said Casca.

"Or something good," said Cassius.

"Will Caesar be king tomorrow?" said Casca.

"If he is," said Cassius, "my sword is ready. I'm a free man and I'll always be free. But perhaps I'm saying too much?"

"No," said Casca, "I'm not afraid. We don't want a king in Rome."

"Give me your hand, Casca," said Cassius. "I've already spoken to some other men," he went on, "Decius, Metellus – you know them. They all think like us."

"And Brutus?"

"I spoke to him."

"The people think Brutus can do no wrong."

"We're going to see Brutus now," said Cassius. "Come with us."

Brutus was in his garden. He walked up and down in the starlight and thought about Caesar.

"There's a war inside me," he said. "There must never be a king of Rome. So – Caesar must die."

He listened to the wind in the trees.

"Suppose Caesar becomes king," he said. "Will he be a bad king? Perhaps not. We can't know. He's never done anything bad to me. But suppose he changes. It's possible. So we must stop him, now. Yes, I think we must."

Lucius, one of his followers, came into the garden.

"Your friend Cassius is here, sir," he said, "and some other men with him."

"Ask them to come here."

"Good morning, Brutus," said Cassius as he came in. "Are we too early?"

"No, I've been awake all night."

"I've brought some friends. You know them all, I think?"

"Give me your hands," said Brutus.

"You know why we're here?" said Cassius.

"Yes."

"Tomorrow's the day," said Cassius, "when Caesar's at the Capitol. Each of us knows what he must do."

"Cassius," said Decius, "what about Antony? Shall we kill him too?"

"No," said Brutus. "One life is enough."

"Decius is right," said Cassius. "Antony's dangerous."

"No, no," said Brutus. "What can he do, when Caesar's dead?"

"He loves Caesar."

"He loves games and sport. Forget him. Come into the house and drink with me," said Brutus.

When Cassius and the other men went away, Portia, the wife of Brutus, came to him.

"Brutus."

"Portia? Why are you up? It's too early."

"What's wrong, Brutus?" said Portia. "You don't eat, or sleep, or talk to me. And who were those men? Tell me. I'm your wife."

"Yes," said Brutus. "You are my true and dearest wife, and I will tell you. But not now, later. Go back to sleep now."

The Ides of March

Caesar's wife, Calpurnia, was unhappy too. "You mustn't leave the house today, Caesar," she said. "Don't go to the Capitol. Something bad is going to happen. You'll die there."

"I'm not afraid of that," said Caesar. "All men must die."

"But don't go out today. Send Antony. He can say you're ill. Please."

But then Decius arrived. "Good morning, Caesar," he said. "I've come to take you to the Capitol. Brutus and the others will be here in a minute."

"He mustn't go today," said Calpurnia.

"Tell them I'm ill, Decius."

"But Caesar," said Decius, "they'll laugh, if I say your wife won't let you come."

"Something bad will happen," said Calpurnia.

"No, no," said Decius. "Something good. They're going to make you king, Caesar. You must come."

"Then I will," said Caesar.

Cassius and Brutus and the others arrived to take Caesar to the Capitol. They went out together, and left Calpurnia alone and afraid.

The fortune-teller waited for Caesar in the street. He had a letter in his hand. "It's all in the letter," he said. "Brutus, Cassius, all of them, they're dangerous. I'll stand here and give this to Caesar as he passes."

Caesar came. He saw the fortune-teller and called out with a smile, "It's the 15th of March, the Ides of March have come."

"Yes, Caesar, but not gone," said the man. "You must read this letter – read it now!"

"What?" said Caesar. "Are you telling Caesar what he must do?"

"Get out of Caesar's way," said Cassius.

They went on to the Capitol. Caesar sat with the other leaders of Rome. "Are we ready?" he said. "Then let the people tell us what we can do for them."

Metellus said, "Caesar, you sent my brother out of Rome. Let him come back."

"No," said Caesar. "What I've done, I've done."

"Caesar," said Casca and Cassius and Decius.

"I said no," said Caesar.

"But Caesar...." said Brutus.

"My answer is no, Brutus."

All the men were round his seat, close to him.

Casca said loudly, "My hands and my sword will speak for me!"

He held up his sword, and brought it down. The others did the same. Brutus was the last.

"You, Brutus?" said Caesar. "Then I will die."

He hid his face, and turned, and fell dead on the ground.

Men, women and children cried and called out and ran. Antony went to his house. Caesar's killers stood close round the body.

"We can say we're Caesar's true friends," said Brutus.

"Now Romans are free men," said Cassius. "In the future, how many men will tell the story of this great day?"

A man came slowly up to them. "I've come from Antony," he said.

"What does Antony say?" said Cassius.

"He says," said the man, " 'Caesar was great, but Brutus is greater. Let me come and talk to you. Tell me why Caesar died. I'm ready to follow Brutus.' "

"Tell Antony to come here," said Brutus. "We won't hurt him." The man went, and Brutus said to Cassius, "Antony's a good man. There's no danger."

"Perhaps," said Cassius.

Antony arrived. Brutus took his hand. Antony looked down at Caesar's dead body, and all the blood. "Oh great Caesar, is this your end?" he said. "So goodbye."

He turned to Brutus. "You can kill me," he said.

"No, Antony, no," said Brutus. "To you, we

must seem the worst men in Rome. And it's true our hands killed Caesar. But in our hearts we loved him. We loved Rome more, that's all. And you shall be our brother."

"And," said Cassius, "you won't lose your money or your land."

"You're right, of course, Brutus," said Antony. "Give me your hands." He took their hands, bloody as they were. Then he said, "Will you let me speak to the people, when Caesar's body goes into the ground?"

"You shall, Antony," said Brutus.

"Brutus," said Cassius quietly. "No. Don't let him speak at the funeral. It's too dangerous."

"Don't be afraid, Cassius," said Brutus. "I'll speak to the people first."

"It's too dangerous," said Cassius again.

Brutus didn't listen to him. He and the others went away, and left Antony alone with Caesar's body.

"I'm quiet now, Caesar," he said. "I've held the hands of your killers. But they won't escape. I'll speak to the people at your funeral and then, and then, the dogs of war shall kill and kill!"

A soldier arrived. "I know you, don't I?" said Antony. "You're from Octavius Caesar, aren't you?" Julius Caesar had no son, and Octavius was the next man in his family. "Tell Octavius he must not come to Rome yet. Tell him to wait."

Brutus Is Never Wrong

All Rome came to Julius Caesar's funeral. Brutus spoke to them first.

"You all loved Caesar. I loved him too. Then why did I kill him? Because I loved Rome more. He was a great soldier, but he wanted to be king. Under a king, people can't be free. So, for you and for Rome, I killed him."

The people listened. They seemed happy enough.

"It's true," they said. "Caesar was a bad man. Brutus is right. We want to be free, don't we?"

"If you want me to die too," said Brutus, "I will."

"No, Brutus, no!" they called. "Live! Be our king! We'll have you for our king!"

Then Antony arrived. He walked slowly and his face was sad. Behind him came men with Caesar's body. Antony went up to Brutus.

"Here's Antony, my friends," said Brutus to the people. "He wants to speak to you. I'm going now. Don't follow me. Stay here with Antony and listen to him."

"He mustn't say anything against you, Brutus," a man called out.

Brutus went, and Antony looked at the people. They were quiet, and he began to speak.

"Friends, Romans, brothers," he began. "Listen to me. Caesar was my dearest friend, always kind, always good. But Brutus said he was dangerous. And, of course, Brutus is never wrong. Brutus says, 'Caesar wanted to be king'. But do you remember? At the sportsfield? You asked Caesar to be your king, three times. And he said, no. He didn't want to be king. But Brutus says he was dangerous and, of course, Brutus is never wrong.''

The people began to talk. "Antony's right," they said.

"Caesar's dead," said Antony. "Will you forget him?"

He stopped. He turned away. His eyes were wet.

"Poor man," said the people.

Antony turned to them again. He said, "Caesar didn't forget you." He showed them a paper. "In this paper," he said, "Caesar has written that you, the Roman people, shall have all his gardens and places where he liked to walk. They will belong to you. And – and," said Antony in a louder voice, "Caesar has given seventy-five pence to every man in Rome: to every man."

Now the people became noisy. "Caesar was a great man," they said. "Brutus killed him! Kill Brutus! Kill them all! Burn their houses!"

They all ran to find Brutus and the others, and Antony was alone with Caesar's body.

He smiled. "Now Octavius can come," he said.

The Dogs of War

The people ran through the streets of Rome; they burned and killed. Many men died, but Brutus and Cassius rode out of the city, and escaped.

Young Octavius Caesar arrived, and he, Antony, and a man called Lepidus, became the three leaders of Rome.

They met to talk about the future. Some men were still dangerous, and they must die.

Octavius's voice was hard and cold. "Your sister's son," he said to Antony. "Yes. He'll die," said Antony. "And your brother," he said to Lepidus. "Kill him," said Lepidus. "And we must look again at Caesar's papers," said Antony. "Seventy-five pence for every man is too much. We'll cut it. And now," he went on, "Brutus and Cassius have an army. We must get ready to fight them."

Brutus and Cassius and their soldiers were in the hills of Sardis, outside Rome. Brutus had bad news from home.

"What is it, Brutus?" said Cassius.

"My wife is dead."

"Portia?"

"She's dead."

"How?" said Cassius.

"I didn't see her before we left Rome. She was afraid for me. She thought she would never see me again. And so, when she was alone in the house...."

"Oh Brutus. This is hard. I'm very sorry."

"Say no more about her," said Brutus. "We must all die." He went on, "You and I are alive and we have work to do. Antony and Octavius and their army are on their way to Philippi. Shall we go to meet them there?"

"No."

"Why not?"

"Let them find us," said Cassius. "Let their soldiers become tired, let their leaders spend their money."

"No," said Brutus.

"Why not?"

"We must go on, to Philippi. I feel this very strongly. It's now or never."

"Then we'll go to Philippi," said Cassius. But he was unhappy about it.

"It's late," said Brutus. "Let's get some sleep. Goodnight, Cassius."

"Goodnight."

Cassius left Brutus alone. "Lucius!" Brutus called out. "Sir?" said Lucius. "Will you play to me?" asked Brutus. "I know you want to sleep, but I'd like some music."

"Yes sir, of course," said Lucius.

The music began. Brutus listened. The light burned low. Lucius fell asleep and then there was no sound.

The ghost of Julius Caesar came.

Brutus looked up and saw it and his blood ran cold.

"What is it, who is it?" he called.

"The man you killed, Brutus."

"Why have you come?"

"To tell you...."

"Yes?"

"You'll see me at Philippi."

The ghost went into the darkness. Brutus called to Lucius.

"Did you see something? Did you hear something?"

"No sir, nothing," said Lucius.

Philippi

On the fields of Philippi, before the fight began, Octavius said to Antony, "You were wrong. You said the enemy wouldn't come down from the hills. But they're here."

Cassius said to Brutus, "Perhaps this is the last time that we shall speak together. If we don't win, what will you do? Will you let Octavius take you to Rome, and show you to the people?"

"Never!" said Brutus. "This day must end the work that began on the Ides of March. We'll say goodbye, Cassius. If we meet again, then we'll smile."

"Goodbye, Brutus. For ever and for ever, goodbye."

The fight was not long.

Later in the day, Cassius thought it was all

over. He said to a soldier, "Pindarus, take my sword, and when I turn my head and shut my eyes, kill me."

Pindarus took the sword, and killed Cassius.

"Caesar," said Cassius as he died, "the sword that killed you, has now killed me."

Cassius died too soon. He was wrong, when he thought the fight was over. Brutus and his soldiers fought Octavius and did well. Brutus came to find Cassius and tell him the good news.

When he saw the body, he said, "Oh Julius Caesar, you are still great and strong. Your ghost is here, and it turns our swords against us. Good-bye, Cassius. I must fight now, but I shall find time to cry for you, I shall find time."

He went back into the fight. He fought hard and long, but in the end, they could not win.

In the evening Brutus sat down with the few followers that were still alive. It was cold, and the sun went down in clouds of blood-red light.

"I've seen the ghost of Julius Caesar again," said Brutus. "I know I shall die here."

He said to his men, "Leave me. Run. Escape if you can." They went. Brutus called to one of them,

"Strato, stay with me."

"Sir?" said Strato.

"Take my sword. Hold it, turn your face away, and let me run on the point. Will you do this for me, Strato?"

"Give me your hand first," said Strato. "Good-

bye, Brutus."

"Goodbye," said Brutus. Strato held the sword, and Brutus ran onto the point. He said as he died, "Ghost of Julius Caesar, be quiet now. I am happier to kill Brutus, than I was to kill you."

Octavius and Antony came to find his body. Antony looked down at the dead Brutus. "This was the greatest of all the Romans," he said. "The others hated Caesar. Brutus loved him, but he loved Rome more. And now he has died like a true Roman. Now all the world can say of him, 'This was a man'."

ANTONY AND CLEOPATRA

A Roman Thought

After Julius Caesar died, Antony, Octavius and Lepidus were the three leaders of the wide Roman world. Antony became the greatest, most famous soldier on earth. He seemed to be, not a man, but a god.

Antony had a Roman wife, Fulvia. But when he went to Egypt, he fell in love with Cleopatra, Queen of Egypt. Antony would not go back to Rome, but stayed in Alexandria with her.

One day, men came from Rome with letters from Octavius. But Antony did not want to hear the news from Rome.

"Antony," said Cleopatra, "read the letters. Perhaps Fulvia is ill. If your wife says you must go, you must go. Or perhaps Octavius Caesar wants you to fight in a war. And if he says you must go, of course you must go."

"Rome can fall into the river Tiber," Antony said. "My place is here. This is the way to live – to love, as you and I love."

"But the letters...."

"No. Let's not talk about it."

"The letters...."

"No. What shall we do this evening?" said Antony. "Shall we walk in the streets and look at the people?"

Later that day, Cleopatra's girls, Charmian and

Iras, and Enobarbus, Antony's friend, listened to a fortune teller.

Charmian said, "Give me a happy future."

"I can't give you a future. I can only see it in your hand," said the fortune-teller.

"Then look at my hand."

"You will be more beautiful than you are now," said the man.

"Oh good. Now tell me I'll marry three kings, and have a son when I'm old, and marry Octavius Caesar and love him, as Antony loves the Queen."

Charmian laughed, but the fortune-teller said, "You will live longer than your queen. But you'll be less happy in the future than you are now."

"Enough," said Charmian. "Tell Iras her future."

"I know my future," said Enobarbus. "I shall go to bed tonight full of drink."

"Tell Iras her future," said Charmian again.

"The same," said the man. "You two girls have the same future."

"How?" said Iras.

"That's all I can say."

"Then go away," said Iras.

The man went, and Cleopatra came in.

"I'm looking for Antony," she said. "Have you seen him, Enobarbus?"

"No, madam."

"He said we'd go out together. But suddenly he had a Roman thought. Find him, Enobarbus."

Antony was with the man from Rome.

"Octavius Caesar is at war with Pompey," said

the man.

"And Antony stays in Egypt," said Antony. "I know what they think of me in Rome. I know what they call Cleopatra. Go on."

"Fulvia, your wife, is dead. Here is the letter."

"Leave me," said Antony. The man went away.

"Fulvia," said Antony.

Enobarbus found him.

"Enobarbus," Antony said, "I must leave Egypt, and soon."

"Oh. Cleopatra will die. She always dies when she hears bad news."

"Fulvia is dead," said Antony.

"What?"

"Fulvia is dead."

"Fulvia?"

"Dead."

Enobarbus smiled. "Thank the gods," he said. "There are other women in the world."

"And Caesar is going to war with Pompey. I've stayed here long enough," said Antony.

Cleopatra still waited for her lover. "Charmian," she said, "Enobarbus hasn't come back. You go and find Antony. And if he seems happy, tell him I'm ill. If he's sad, tell him I'm dancing."

"Madam," said Charmian, "that's not the way to keep a lover."

"Oh?" said Cleopatra. "What must I do?"

"Always do what he wants. Never go against him."

"Wrong," said Cleopatra. "That's the way to

lose him."

Antony arrived.

"I'm very ill," said Cleopatra. She didn't look at him.

"I'm sorry, my dearest Queen," said Antony.

"Go away."

"What's wrong?"

"I know you have good news from Rome," said Cleopatra. "Fulvia wants you to go home."

"Cleopatra...."

"You haven't been true to Fulvia. You won't be true to me, either."

"Cleopatra...."

"Oh say goodbye and go."

"Listen, will you listen!" said Antony. "Caesar is going to war with Pompey. I must go and fight. And don't be afraid of Fulvia. She's dead."

"What? Can Fulvia die?"

"It's true."

"And you're not crying for her? Now I know how you'll be when I'm dead."

"Enough, Cleopatra. You shall tell me what to do. Go? Or stay here?"

"You must go to Rome, of course, Antony," she said. "All my love goes with you."

"You'll always be with me, Cleopatra," said Antony. "You'll stay here, but I'll take you with me. I'll go, but I'll still be here with you."

Rome

Antony went to Rome to talk to Octavius and Lepidus. Enobarbus went with him.

"I hope," said Lepidus before the meeting, "that Antony will be friendly to Caesar."

"Antony will do what he pleases," said Enobarbus.

"Sit down," said Caesar.

"Sir, after you."

They sat down.

"I know you're not pleased with me because I stayed in Egypt," said Antony.

"No," said Caesar. "I'm not pleased."

"But that's not your business, Caesar. It's mine."

"Is it?"

"Yes," said Antony.

"I wrote to you," said Caesar. "You didn't read my letters."

"I read them."

"You once said," said Caesar, "you'd always help me in a new war."

"I've come to Rome, haven't I?"

"Enough," said Enobarbus. "There isn't time for this. Pompey's waiting for you."

"Enobarbus," said Antony, and looked at him.

"Not another word," said Enobarbus. "I'll be a stone."

"I want us to be friends, Antony," said Caesar. "But how? What will keep us together?"

"There's one way," said Lepidus. "Antony has no wife now."

"Don't tell Cleopatra," said Enobarbus.

"I'm not married, Caesar," said Antony.

"Marry Octavia, Caesar's sister," said Lepidus. "Then you'll belong to Caesar's family."

"Antony?" said Caesar.

"Will Octavia marry me?"

"Yes," said Caesar.

"Then I'll marry her."

"Give me your hand," said Caesar. "Now: Pompey."

Enobarbus's Roman friends asked him about Cleopatra.

"What's she like?" they said. "Beautiful?"

"Truly, most lovely," said Enobarbus. "The most beautiful woman in the world."

"How did they fall in love?"

"He saw her when she came up the river Nile in her boat. She asked him to dinner, he went, and paid for his dinner with his heart."

"But he'll leave her now."

"Never," said Enobarbus. "He can't. She's not young, but age can't change her. She's not one woman, she's a hundred. He'll go back to her."

Antony married Octavia. He was kind to her, but he thought about Cleopatra all the time. He said, "My happiness is in the East, Enobarbus."

"Yes. I know. Octavia's good, but she's cold.

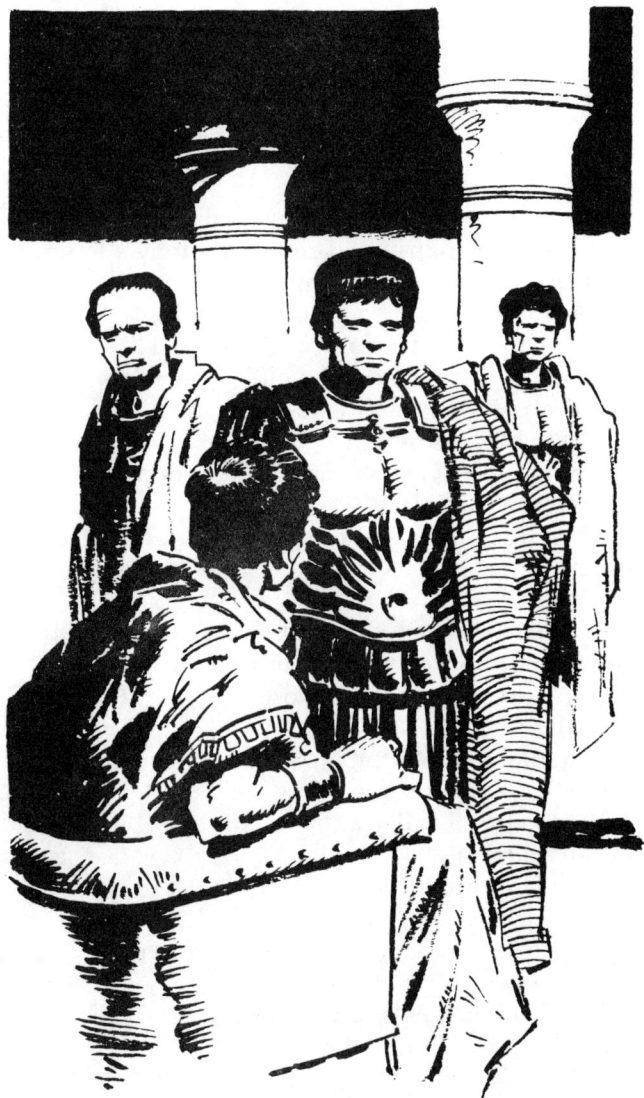

And the beds in the East are soft."

Alexandria

In Alexandria Cleopatra waited for news of Antony. The man who brought Antony's letters from Rome came with a long face.

"Antony's dead?" said Cleopatra.

"No, madam. He's not dead, or sick."

"Here's some gold for you," said Cleopatra. "And are Antony and Caesar friends?"

"Yes. But madam...."

"But?" said Cleopatra. "But? Antony's well, he's free. What else?"

"Not free, madam. I didn't say that. He's married."

"What?"

"Married to Octavia, Caesar's sister."

Cleopatra screamed at him. "You shall die, you'll lose your eyes, you'll lose your hair, I'll cook you alive!"

"Madam," cried the man, "I only brought the news. I didn't make it."

"Go before I kill you!"

The man ran.

"Oh Charmian," said Cleopatra. "I'm going to die. Help me, help me."

But then she said, "Call the man back."

He came.

"This Octavia," said Cleopatra. "Have you seen her?"

"Yes, great Queen."

"Is she tall, like me?"

"She is not, madam."

"How old is she?"

"She's old, madam. About thirty."

"And her face?"

"It's round, madam."

"Not a good face. Her hair?"

"Brown, madam. Not bright."

"Here's some gold for you. I have some letters for Antony; you can take them to Rome. Go and get ready."

"A nice man," said Charmian, after he went.

"Yes. Octavia's not beautiful. Or young."

"Oh no, madam."

"Good."

Think and Die

Rome didn't go to war with Pompey. Caesar, Antony and Lepidus met him, talked with him, and drank with him. He took his army home.

But Caesar and Antony could not be friends for long. Antony went back to Alexandria. Then Caesar made ready for another war, against Antony and Cleopatra this time.

Cleopatra wanted to lead her soldiers to war.

"You can't," said Enobarbus.

"Why not?"

"Because it's not right," he said. "Is it? Is it? Antony's heart and his thoughts will be with you.

He can't fight if you're in danger. They're already laughing in Rome. They say Caesar's going to war against a lot of Egyptian women."

"Rome can fall in little pieces."

Antony arrived.

"We'll fight at sea, Enobarbus," he said.

"At sea? Why? Why? Why?"

"Caesar thinks we can't."

"Caesar's right," said Enobarbus. "You haven't enough men, your ships are heavy and Caesar's are light and fast. His men have fought at sea many times. Yours haven't. You can win on land, but not at sea."

"I'll fight at sea," said Antony.

"Egypt has ships," said Cleopatra. "More than enough."

Enobarbus was right. Antony did not win. In the middle of the fight, Cleopatra with her ships suddenly turned and left. Antony followed her, and Caesar won.

After this, many of Antony's followers went to Caesar. Enobarbus stayed, but he said, "I'm staying because Antony's my old friend. He won't ever win a fight again. This is the end of the greatest soldier in the world."

Antony was very unhappy. "Long ago, at Philippi," he said to Cleopatra, "I was a good soldier. Young Octavius knew nothing then." He looked at Cleopatra. "Where have you led me, Egyptian Queen? You know very well that if you run, I must follow. Didn't you know that?"

"I'm sorry, I'm sorry," said Cleopatra. "Did

you send a letter to Caesar? What did you say?"

"I asked him to let me stay in Egypt; not as a soldier, but as a man like other men."

Caesar did not answer Antony. He wrote to Cleopatra and said that she could stay in Egypt and still be queen. But she must either send Antony away, or kill him.

"What shall we do, Enobarbus?" said Cleopatra.

"Think, and die," said Enobarbus.

Strange Music

Caesar brought an army to Alexandria and another war began.

"Antony hasn't a hope," said Enobarbus. "The time of his greatness is over. I'll find a way to leave him. Why not? He won't listen to me. I can't help him."

The night before the fight began, soldiers in the streets of Alexandria heard strange music, in the air and under the earth. "What does it mean?" said one. "Nothing good," said another. "The gods loved Antony. Now they're leaving him."

In the morning Antony said to Cleopatra, "You shall see me fight well today. One kiss, a soldier's kiss, and I must leave you."

"Come madam," said Charmian and Iras when Antony went. "We can only wait."

There was bad news for Antony that morning. A soldier brought it.

"Enobarbus has left you, and gone to Caesar," he said.

"Gone to Caesar?"

"Yes sir. He's left all his money and treasure here."

"Send it to him," said Antony. "I'll write a letter to go with it. Oh – how many good men have fallen because of me! Enobarbus."

Enobarbus was with Caesar's army when the soldier brought Antony's letter. "He's sent all your treasure," said the man.

"I give it to you," said Enobarbus. "Oh," he said when the man went, "Antony is still a god. And I am the worst man in the world. The sun is hot, but I feel cold and sick. I'm going to die."

Enobarbus found a place, far from the fight, and there he died.

In the beginning, Antony did well. Caesar's soldiers ran. That night Antony came home to Cleopatra and smiled at her.

"Oh Antony," she said. "Have you escaped from the world, and come back to me?"

"My sweet bird," said Antony, "I know my hair is grey; but still, my girl, I can fight better than any young man. Give me your hand. Tonight we'll all walk together, you and I and our soldiers. We'll walk through Alexandria, and the sound of music shall fill the earth and sky."

Next day, Antony said, "Caesar is going to fight at sea today. His ships are ready. We didn't please him when we fought on land."

The Long Day's Work Is Over

At the end of this day, Antony lost everything. He cried out, "The Egyptian woman has sold me to the boy Caesar. All my men have gone to Caesar. They're drinking with him now, like old friends. I shall not see tomorrow's sun. I have nothing, nothing, nothing."

Cleopatra came to him.

"Go," he said to her. "Caesar can have you, and take you to Rome, and show you to the people."

Cleopatra cried and ran from him.

"She shall die," said Antony. "She shall die."

Cleopatra went to Charmian and Iras. "Help me, help me," she said. "I didn't sell him, I didn't! What shall I do? Caesar will come for me!"

Charmian said, "You have a Monument, madam. You can go there, and close all the doors, and be safe. Then, send a man to tell Antony you're dead. Don't cry, don't cry."

They went to the Monument, a stone building where her body would go when she died. She sent a soldier to Antony.

"The woman has sold me," Antony said to him.

"No," said the man. "She loved you."

"She shall die."

"She can only die once, Antony. She's dead now. Her last word was Antony."

"Dead?"

"Dead."

"Now I'll take off my sword. The long day's work is over, and I must sleep. Cleopatra, I'll come to you, my Queen. Wait for me, wait. Hand in hand we'll walk in flowery fields, and all the dead will smile at us."

Antony called Eros, one of the few old friends that were left in Alexandria. "Eros, you must help me," he said. "Do you want Caesar to take me to Rome, and show me to the people?"

"No," said Eros, "but I can't kill you, Antony."

"You must."

"Then turn your face away from mine, that face the whole world knew."

"I will."

"Let me say goodbye, Antony."

"Goodbye, Eros. Now!"

But Eros put the sword point into his own heart, and died.

Antony took the sword. "I'll die alone," he said. The sword went into his body, and he fell, but he was not dead.

Another soldier came from Cleopatra, and found him.

"Kill me," said Antony. "Kill me."

"Cleopatra sent me," said the man. "She isn't dead, sir. She told you she was, but then she was afraid, and sent me to you."

"Too late," said Antony. "But call some men, and carry me to Cleopatra, and I will thank you."

We'll Die Like Romans

At the top of the Monument, Cleopatra waited. She looked down and saw Antony. He was on the ground, and there was blood on his clothes.

"Oh sun," she said. "Burn the sky, let the whole world stay in darkness. Charmian, help, Iras, help me. Help, you friends below. Bring him to me."

"I am dying, Egypt, dying," said Antony. "I'm waiting only to kiss you for the last time. Come down to me."

"Caesar's men will take me if I come to you my love," she said. "Help me, Charmian and Iras, we must get him up to us."

They lifted him up to Cleopatra.

"One kiss," she said, with her arm round him. "Now you can die where you have lived."

"Don't cry, Cleopatra. I'm going. I can do no more." He kissed her, and was dead.

"Oh Queen of Egypt," said Iras.

"Not a queen now," said Cleopatra, "but a poor woman, like any other woman. I'll not stay long on earth without him. Come, you and I will do what's right, what's good, we'll die like Romans."

"Yes," said Iras. "Finish, madam. The bright day is done, and we are going into darkness."

"Charmian," said Cleopatra, "I spoke to one of my Egyptians. He's bringing me some little

snakes, deadly snakes from the river Nile. He'll hide them in a box of fruit. Now dress me like a Queen. I'm going to Antony."

Charmian helped her to dress. The Egyptian brought the fruit, with the snakes under it.

Cleopatra took a snake. She let it bite her.

"Antony's calling me," she said. "Husband, I'm coming. Goodbye, kind Charmian and Iras, a long goodbye."

"Oh, my heart," said Iras. "My heart!" She fell to the ground.

"She's dead, madam," said Charmian.

"Is it so easy to die?" said Cleopatra. "She'll meet Antony before me."

"Oh star of the East," said Charmian. "Ssh – I'm going to sleep," said Cleopatra.

Her eyes closed. Charmian took a snake, and let it bite her.

Caesar came with soldiers. "The queen?" they said.

"Asleep," said Charmian.

"What's this? She's dead, Charmian?"

"She died like a queen. Oh!" Then Charmian fell, and died beside her queen and Iras.

"Cleopatra shall lie in the ground with her Antony," said Caesar. "All the world shall tell the story of these two great lovers."

A Word Game

Do you like to play games with words?
Here's a game for you now. There are 41
questions, and all the answers come from the
story.

Write down the *first letter* of every answer. At the
end, all those letters make words.

An American writer wrote them. Can you read
them?

1 Pindarus ____ Cassius.
2 The 15th day of March.
3 Calpurnia was the ____ of Caesar's wife.
4 On holidays the Romans played ____ .
5 Julius Caesar was a great Roman ____ .
6 Antony said, "The ____ of war shall kill and
   kill."
7 Antony married her.
8 A river in Egypt.
9 Antony sent all Enobarbus's ____ to him.
10 Cleopatra ____ a snake bite her.
11 One of Cleopatra's girls.
12 Only Brutus heard the ____ of Caesar's
   ghost.
13 Cleopatra was Queen of ____ .
14 He became one of the three leaders of Rome.
15 Another of Rome's three leaders.
16 Did Antony help to kill Caesar?
17 Caesar left all his ____ to the people.

18 Antony and Cleopatra were very much
    ____ love.
19 A ____ -teller told Caesar of danger.
20 Rome was on this river.
21 When Caesar came home, Rome took a ____ .
22 Antony's friend in Egypt.
23 Brutus's wife.
24 Charmian called Cleopatra "Star of the
    ____ ."
25 Octavia was about 30 years ____ .
26 Caesar gave 75 ____ to every man in Rome.
27 In Egypt, Antony did not read the ____ from
    Octavius.
28 Antony asked ____ to kill him.
29 The men killed Caesar with their ____
30 Caesar: "All the world shall ____ the story of
    these two great lovers."
31 He spoke to the people at Caesar's funeral.
32 Caesar died in this city.
33 On the holiday, Caesar and his friends
    walked ____ the streets.
34 Cassius thought Caesar was a ____ , sick old
    man.
35 Octavia's was brown.
36 Caesar didn't want to go to the Capitol: "Tell
    them I'm ____ ."
37 Octavia was Caesar's daughter: *true* or *not
    true?*
38 Caesar wanted to become one.
39 Cleopatra lived ____ Alexandria.
40 Was it *day* or *night* when the killers met in
    Brutus's garden.
41 The ____ of dead Caesar came to Brutus.

Answers

1 killed 2 Ides 3 name 4 games 5 soldier
6 dogs 7 Octavia 8 Nile 9 treasure 10 let
11 Iras 12 voice 13 Egypt 14 Lepidus
15 Octavius 16 no 17 gardens 18 in
19 fortune 20 Tiber 21 holiday 22 Enobarbus
23 Portia 24 East 25 old 26 pence 27 letters
28 Eros 29 swords 30 tell 31 Antony
32 Rome 33 through 34 tired 35 hair 36 ill
37 not true 38 king 39 in 40 night 41 ghost